This book belongs to

~~BAT~~

_____

FOR ELLIE
(MY FELLOW FOOD FIEND)
x

First published 2017 by Two Hoots
This edition published 2018 by Two Hoots
an imprint of Pan Macmillan
20 New Wharf Road, London N1 9RR
Associated companies throughout the world
www.panmacmillan.com
Text and illustrations copyright © Morag Hood 2017
Moral rights asserted.

1 3 5 7 9 8 6 4 2
A CIP catalogue record for this book is available from the British Library.
Printed in China
The illustrations in this book were created using lino print and collage.

www.twohootsbooks.com

MORAG HOOD

I AM BAT

TWO HOOTS

I AM BAT.

I do not like mornings.

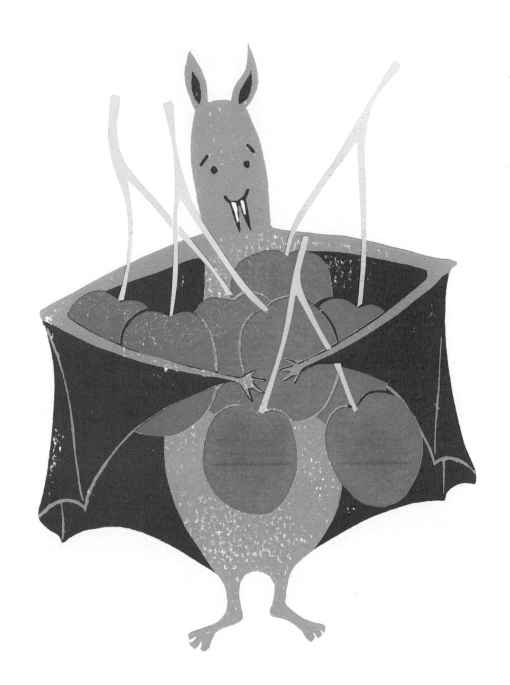

I like **CHERRIES.**

They are my

FAVOURITE

of all things.

They are

 JUICY and  RED

and

DELICIOUS

...THEY ARE MINE.

Do **NOT**

take my cherries.

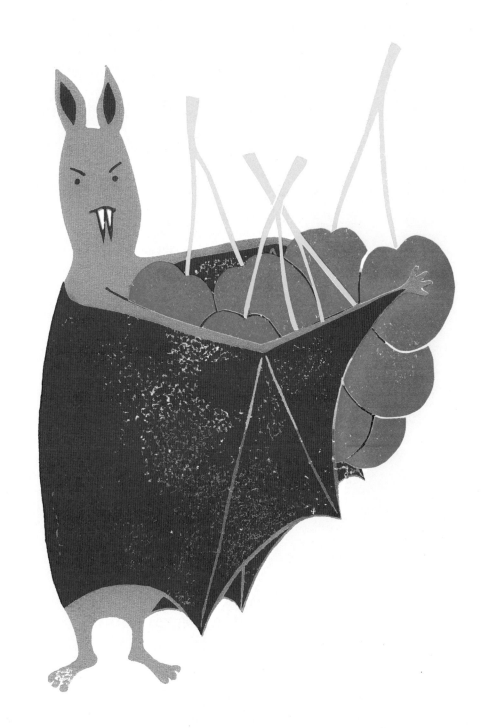

If you take my

cherries

I will be

ANGRY.

I will be **FEROCIOUS** like a lion.

(But smaller and with wings.)

I will just

leave my

cherries

here.

DO

NOT

touch

them.

I WILL KNOW IF
YOU TAKE ONE.

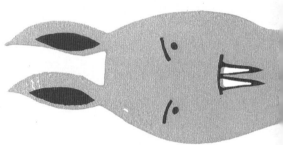

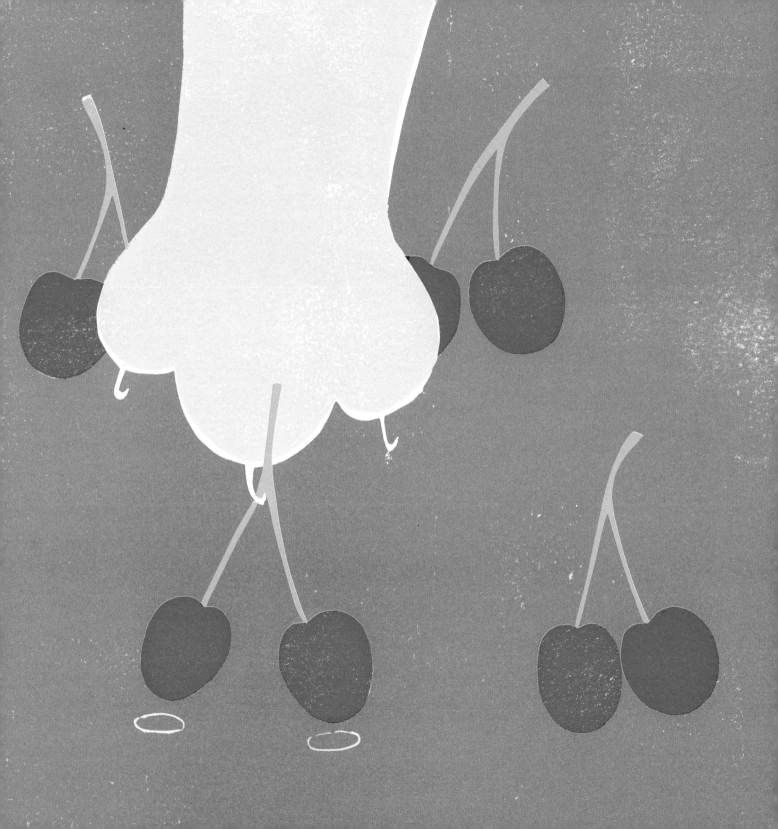

My
CHERRIES!
Some of them are
MISSING.

Where did
they go?

Was it

YOU?

I will

NEVER

be happy again.

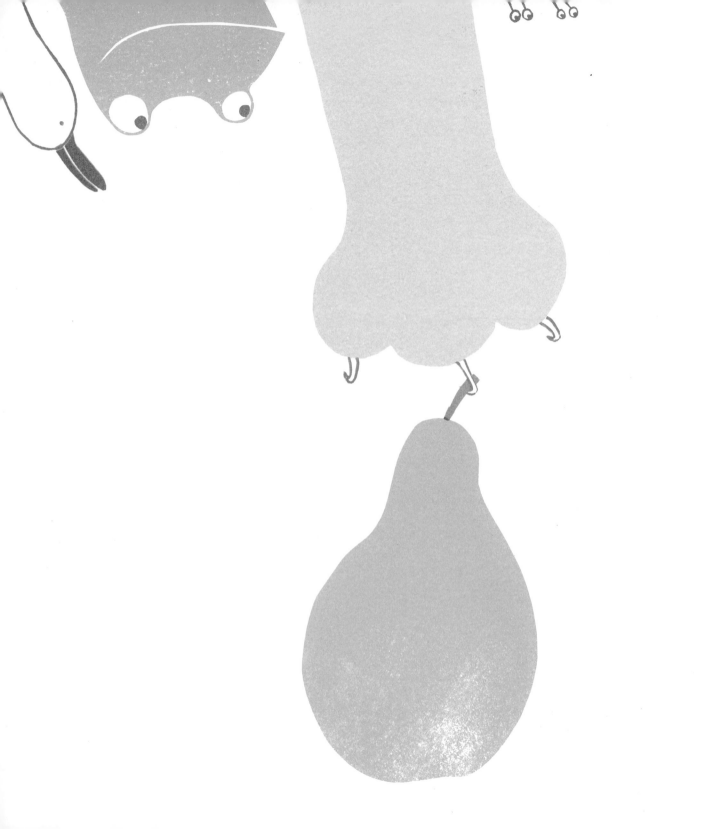

Ooh . . .

A PEAR!

I like **PEARS.**

I AM
BAT.

DO
NOT
TAKE
MY
PEAR.

Bat's recipe for

JUICY RED DELICIOUS CHERRIES

Ingredients

Cherries

Method

Take one cherry and add another cherry.
Mix.
Taste.
Add a lot more cherries.
Check for lions.
Serve.

Serves one.